Cambridge Young Learners
English Tests

Cambridge Movers 7

Answer Booklet

Examination papers from

University of Cambridge
ESOL Examinations:

English for Speakers of Other Languages

CAMBRIDGE
UNIVERSITY PRESS

CAMBRIDGE UNIVERSITY PRESS
Cambridge, New York, Melbourne, Madrid, Cape Town,
Singapore, São Paulo, Delhi, Mexico City

Cambridge University Press
The Edinburgh Building, Cambridge CB2 8RU, UK

www.cambridge.org
Information on this title: www.cambridge.org/9780521173728

First published 2011
4th printing 2013

Printed in Poland by Opolgraf

A catalogue record for this publication is available from the British Library

ISBN 978-0-521-17371-1 Student's Book
ISBN 978-0-521-17372-8 Answer Booklet
ISBN 978-0-521-17373-5 Audio CD

Cover design by David Lawton
Produced by Peter & Jan Simmonett

Contents

Introduction

The *Cambridge Young Learners English Tests* offer an elementary-level testing system (up to CEFR level A2) for learners of English between the ages of 7 and 12. The tests include 3 key levels of assessment: *Starters*, *Movers* and *Flyers*.

Movers is the second level in the system. Test instructions are very simple and consist only of words and structures specified in the syllabus.

The complete test lasts about an hour and has the following components: Listening, Reading and Writing, and Speaking.

	length	number of parts	number of questions
Listening	approx. 25 minutes	5	25
Reading and Writing	30 minutes	6	40
Speaking	approx. 5–7 minutes	4	–

Candidates need a pen or pencil for the Reading and Writing paper, and coloured pens or pencils for the Listening paper. All answers are written on the question papers.

Listening

In general, the aim is to focus on the 'here and now' and to use language in meaningful contexts. In addition to multiple-choice and short-answer questions, candidates are asked to use coloured pencils to mark their responses to one task. There are 5 parts. Each part begins with a clear example.

part	main skill focus	input	expected response	number of questions
1		picture, names and dialogue	draw lines to match names to people in a picture	5
2	the main skill focus in all five parts of the Listening test is listening for specific information of various kinds, e.g. numbers, describing people etc.	form or page of notepad with missing words and dialogue	write words or numbers in gaps	5
3		pictures, days of the week and dialogue	draw lines from days of week to correct pictures	5
4		3-option multiple-choice pictures and dialogues	tick boxes under correct picture	5
5		picture and dialogue	carry out instructions to colour, draw and write (range of colours is: black, blue, brown, green, grey, orange, pink, purple, red, yellow)	5

Reading and Writing

Again, the focus is on the 'here and now' and the use of language in meaningful contexts where possible. To complete the test, candidates need a single pen or pencil of any colour. There are 6 parts, each starting with a clear example.

part	main skill focus	input	expected response	number of items
1	reading short definitions and matching to words writing words	labelled pictures and definitions	copy the correct words next to the definitions	6
2	reading sentences about a picture and writing one-word answers	1 picture and sentences	write 'yes'/'no'	6
3	reading a dialogue and choosing the correct responses	1 picture and short dialogue with multiple-choice responses	choose correct response by circling a letter	6
4	reading for specific information and gist copying words	cloze text, words and pictures	choose and copy missing words correctly; tick a box to choose the best title for the story	7
5	reading a story and completing sentences about the story	story, pictures and gapped sentences	complete sentences about the story by writing 1, 2 or 3 words	10
6	reading and understanding a factual text copying words	gapped text and 3-option multiple choice (grammatical words)	complete text by selecting the correct words and copying them in corresponding gaps	5

Speaking

In the Speaking test, the candidate speaks with 1 examiner for about 6 minutes. The format of the test is explained in advance to the child in their native language by a teacher or person familiar to them. This person then takes the child into the exam room and introduces them to the examiner.

Speaking ability is assessed according to various criteria, including comprehension, the ability to produce an appropriate response and pronunciation.

part	main skill focus	input	expected response
1	describing two pictures by using short responses	two similar pictures	identify four differences between pictures
2	understanding the beginning of a story and then continuing it based on a series of pictures	picture sequence	describe each picture in turn
3	suggesting a picture which is different and explaining why	picture sets	identify the odd one out and give reason
4	understanding and responding to personal questions	open-ended questions about candidate	answer personal questions

Further information

The topics, structures, words and tasks upon which the *Cambridge Young Learners English Tests* are based are comprehensively described in the Handbook, so teachers or parents can know exactly what to expect.

Further information about the *Cambridge Young Learners English Tests* can be obtained from the Centre Exams Manager for Cambridge ESOL examinations in your area, or from:

University of Cambridge ESOL Examinations
1 Hills Road
Cambridge
CB1 2EU
United Kingdom

Telephone: +44 1223 553997
Fax: +44 1223 553621

e-mail: ESOLHelpdesk@CambridgeESOL.org
www.CambridgeESOL.org

Test 1 Answers

Listening

Part 1 (5 marks)

Lines should be drawn between:

1 Kim and the man painting a window
2 Vicky and the girl carrying a box of vegetables
3 Jack and the boy with the bike
4 Anna and the girl playing with a ball on the mat
5 Daisy and the girl climbing a tree

Part 2 (5 marks)

1 swimming 2 afternoon(s) 3 Hart (correct spelling)
4 (her father's/dad's) car 5 tennis

Part 3 (5 marks)

1 Thursday – film about girl and helicopter
2 Saturday – kite and walk with dog in forest
3 Monday – picnic and photo of lizard in forest
4 Tuesday – beach and swam in sea
5 Sunday – beach and took photos of dog

Part 4 (5 marks)

1 B 2 B 3 A 4 A 5 C

Part 5 (5 marks)

1 Colour the waterfall near the woman – yellow
2 Colour the head of the man in the lake – purple
3 Colour the coconuts on the tree – orange
4 Colour the bigger hippo in the lake – green
5 Draw a rock next to the flowers

TRANSCRIPT *Hello. This is the Cambridge Movers Practice Listening Test, Test 1.*

Part 1 *Look at Part 1. Look at the picture. Listen and look. There is one example.*

[pause]

WOMAN: What a lot of people in your garden today. Who's the boy who's running?
BOY: The boy playing with the cat?
WOMAN: Yes.
BOY: That's Tom. He's my cousin.

[pause]

Can you see the line? This is an example.
Now you listen and draw lines.

[pause]

1

WOMAN: Who's painting the window?
BOY: That's Kim.
WOMAN: It looks difficult.
BOY: Yes, but he likes painting.

[pause]

2

WOMAN: Look at that girl!
BOY: That's Vicky. She's carrying a box.
WOMAN: Are there vegetables in the box?
BOY: Yes, they come from her garden. She brings them every week.

[pause]

3

WOMAN: And the boy with the bike. Who's he?
BOY: That's Jack – he's my brother's friend. It's a new bike.
WOMAN: Mmm. It looks great.
BOY: Yes. His grandpa gave it to him last week.

[pause]

4

WOMAN: There are two children who are sitting on a mat. Who's the girl?
BOY: Oh, that's Anna and that's her brother.
WOMAN: They're enjoying their game.
BOY: Yes, they are!

[pause]

5

WOMAN: Who's climbing the tree?
BOY: That's Daisy.
WOMAN: She's very good at climbing.
BOY: Yes, she isn't afraid. She does that every day.

[pause]

Now listen to Part 1 again.

[The recording is repeated.]

[pause]

That is the end of Part 1.

[pause]

Part 2 *Listen and look. There is one example.*

[pause]

MAN: Hello. Can I ask you some questions about classes at the sports centre, please?
GIRL: OK.
MAN: First. What's your name?
GIRL: Lucy Flynn.
MAN: Lucy Flynn. Is that F-L-Y double N?
GIRL: That's right.

[pause]

Can you see the answer? Now you listen and write.

[pause]

1

MAN: Right, Lucy, which classes do you go to here?
GIRL: I have a swimming class.
MAN: Swimming, OK. And do you enjoy that?
GIRL: Very much.
MAN: Good.

[pause]

2

MAN: When do you have your class, Lucy?
GIRL: On Saturday morning – no, that's wrong. It's in the afternoon now.
MAN: OK, and you have it every week?
GIRL: Yes, on Saturday afternoon.

[pause]

3

MAN: What's the name of your teacher?
GIRL: It's Mr Hart. He's very nice.
MAN: Do you spell that H-A-R-T?
GIRL: Yes, that's right.
MAN: Great.

[pause]

4

MAN: Now, how do you get here, Lucy?
GIRL: I come with my father in the car.
MAN: Does he come in and watch the class?
GIRL: No, he sits in the car and reads his book!

[pause]

5

MAN: Now the last question. Do you do a lot of sports?
GIRL: Yes, I play tennis, hockey and basketball.
MAN: And which is your favourite?
GIRL: Oh, I like tennis best.
MAN: Thank you very much, Lucy.

[pause]

Now listen to Part 2 again.

[The recording is repeated.]

[pause]

That is the end of Part 2.

[pause]

Part 3 *Look at the pictures. What did Ben do last week?*
Listen and look. There is one example.

[pause]

WOMAN: Were you on holiday last week, Ben?
BOY: Yes, on Wednesday I went to see my uncle and aunt.
WOMAN: Did you go by train?
BOY: No, we went in a helicopter because they live on an island.
WOMAN: Wow!

[pause]

Can you see the line from the word Wednesday? On Wednesday, Ben went to visit his uncle and aunt.
Now you listen and draw lines.

[pause]

1

WOMAN: So, Ben, what did you do on holiday?
BOY: Well, on Thursday evening we went to the cinema.
WOMAN: On Thursday? Did you see that great new film about the boy with a dog that can speak?
BOY: No. It was about a girl and a helicopter. It was very exciting.
WOMAN: Oh.

[pause]

2

BOY: There's a big forest next to my uncle's house.
WOMAN: Did you go there on Friday?
BOY: No, we went on Saturday.
WOMAN: Oh,
BOY: We took a kite and we also took the dog for a walk.

[pause]

3

BOY: Then we went to the forest again on Monday.
WOMAN: And what did you do there?
BOY: We had a picnic and took some photos.
WOMAN: Did you enjoy it?
BOY: Yes, I took a good picture of some lizards.

[pause]

4

WOMAN: Did you go to the cinema again another day?
BOY: No, the weather was nice. On Tuesday we went to the beach.
WOMAN: Did you go in the sea?
BOY: Well, I did, but my aunt and uncle didn't.
WOMAN: What about the dog?
BOY: He doesn't like water. He likes playing on the sand. Tuesday was a good day.

[pause]

5

WOMAN: I'd like to see their dog.
BOY: I've got some pictures. Look.
WOMAN: Oh, he looks happy.
BOY: Yes, we went to the beach again on Sunday and I took some photos of him there. It was a cold day.
WOMAN: Yes, I can see there aren't any people in the sea.

[pause]

Now listen to Part 3 again.

[The recording is repeated.]

[pause]

That is the end of Part 3.

[pause]

Part 4 *Look at the pictures. Listen and look. There is one example.*

[pause]

What did Tony eat at his party?

[pause]

BOY: Hi, Aunt Sally.
WOMAN: Did you have a nice birthday, Tony?
BOY: Yes, it was great.
WOMAN: What did you have to eat at the party?
BOY: We had burgers.
WOMAN: And chips?
BOY: No, but we had lots of ice cream.

[pause]

Can you see the tick? Now you listen and tick the box.

[pause]

1 Which pet did Tony get for his birthday?

WOMAN: Did you get a snake for your birthday, Tony?
BOY: No, I wanted one but Mum doesn't like them.
WOMAN: Oh dear. My children don't like spiders, but I do.
BOY: So do I. Mum bought me a rabbit. It's OK.
WOMAN: Can I see it?
BOY: Yes.

[pause]

2 What did Tony wear at his party?

WOMAN: That's a nice shirt that you're wearing.
BOY: Yes, it was a present from a friend.
WOMAN: And at the party did you wear the sweater that I bought you?
BOY: It was too hot. I wore a T-shirt.

[pause]

3 What did the children do at the party?

WOMAN: What did you do at your party?
BOY: We played some good games. We had to look for treasure.
WOMAN: Did you have a map to look at?
BOY: Yes.
WOMAN: And did you play football?
BOY: No, but after the party I went skating with my brother.

[pause]

4 What did Tony like best about his birthday?

WOMAN: What did you like best about your birthday, Tony?

BOY: Well, I like this watch and Dad gave me a computer.

WOMAN: Wow! What a lot of presents!

BOY: Yes, but I made a video of the party. That was the best thing.

[pause]

5 What's the matter with Tony?

WOMAN: But what's the matter, Tony? Have you got a headache?

BOY: No. I ate too much birthday cake yesterday.

WOMAN: Have you got a stomach ache then? I'm sorry.

BOY: No, but I've got a toothache. It hurts a lot.

[pause]

Now listen to Part 4 again.

[The recording is repeated.]

[pause]

That is the end of Part 4.

[pause]

Part 5   *Look at the picture. Listen and look. There is one example.*

[pause]

MAN: Hello, May. Would you like to make this picture look better?

GIRL: Yes, please.

MAN: OK. First, look at the moon.

GIRL: I can see it. Can I colour it?

MAN: Yes. Colour the moon blue.

[pause]

Can you see the blue moon? This is an example. Now you listen and colour and draw.

[pause]

1

GIRL: OK, what shall I do now?

MAN: Can you see the woman?

GIRL: Yes, she's standing next to the waterfall.

MAN: Yes, well, colour that waterfall yellow.

GIRL: OK.

[pause]

2

MAN: Look, there's a man in the lake.

GIRL: Yes, I can see him.

MAN: Colour his head purple.

GIRL: The man's head. OK, I'm colouring that now.

[pause]

3

GIRL: And look at that tree!

MAN: Yes, it has some coconuts on it.

GIRL: Can I colour them orange?

MAN: That's a good idea. I like coconuts, do you?

GIRL: Yes, they're good to eat.

[pause]

4

MAN: Now, the hippo in the lake. Colour that.

GIRL: Well, there are two. Which one?

MAN: The bigger one. Make it green.

GIRL: OK, the bigger hippo in the lake.

[pause]

5

MAN: Now you can do some drawing.

GIRL: OK. Shall I put a rock in the picture?

MAN: Yes, draw a rock next to the flowers.

GIRL: Umm. Next to the flowers. I like the picture now.

[pause]

Now listen to Part 5 again

[The recording is repeated.]

[pause]

That is the end of the Movers Practice Listening Test 1.

Reading and Writing

Part 1 (6 marks)

1 DVDs   2 soup   3 music
4 pears   5 coffee   6 a party

Part 2 (6 marks)

1 yes   2 yes   3 no   4 no   5 yes   6 no

Part 3 (6 marks)

1 A   2 A   3 B   4 A   5 C   6 C

Part 4 (7 marks)

1 fields   2 carrots   3 rode   4 surprised
5 hold   6 smiled   7 Some new friends for Fred

Part 5 (10 marks)

1 hot/sunny   2 Sunday   3 towel   4 door
5 kitchen   6 (big) (green) crocodile   7 Sally
8 hide/stay inside   9 mum and dad   10 back

Part 6 (5 marks)

1 lots   2 There   3 the   4 too   5 learn

Speaking

Part	Examiner does this:	Examiner says this:	Minimum response expected from child:	Back-up questions:
	Usher brings candidate in.	Usher to examiner: **Hello. This is (child's name*).** Examiner: **Hello, *. My name's *Jane*/*Ms Smith*.** **How old are you, *?**	**Hello.** *nine*	**Are you *nine*/*ten*?**
1	Points to **Find the differences** pictures.	**Look at these pictures. They look the same, but some things are different. Here there are two trees, but here there are three trees.** **What other different things can you see?**	Describes four other differences: • long/short hair • panda/kangaroo • bird/no bird • kicking/holding ball	Point to other differences the candidate does not mention. Give first half of response: **Here the woman has long hair, but here …**
2	Points to **Picture Story**. Allows time to look at the pictures.	**Now look at these pictures. They show a story. It's called 'Children like painting'. Just look at the pictures first. (Pause.) Look at the first one.** **The girls are painting in the living room. Mum's helping them and their baby brother's watching them.** **Now you tell the story.** (pointing at the other pictures)	(Many variations possible) *Mum's talking on the phone.* *Now the baby's painting the wall.* *Mum's pointing to the wall. She isn't happy.*	Questions to prompt other parts of the story: **What's Mum doing now?** **What's the baby doing now?** **What's Mum doing? Is she happy?**

* Remember to use the child's name throughout the test.

Part	Examiner does this:	Examiner says this:	Minimum response expected from child:	Back-up questions:
3	Points to **Odd-one-out** pictures.	**Now look at these four pictures. One is different. The book is different. A lemon, a pineapple and an orange are fruit. You eat them. You don't eat a book. You read it.**		
	Points to the second, third and fourth sets of pictures in turn.	**Now you tell me about these pictures. Which one is different? (Why?)**	Candidate suggests a difference (any plausible difference is acceptable).	**These are all ....?** (dirty) **And this is ... ?** (clean) **What are these?** (cars) **And this?** (horse) **Where are these children playing?** (outside) **And these children?** (inside)
4	Puts away all pictures.	**Now let's talk about your weekend.**		
		Where do you go at the weekend?	*park*	**Do you go to the *park*?**
		What games do you play at the weekend?	*computer games*	**Do you play *computer games*?**
		Who do you play with?	*(my) friend*	**Do you play with *your friend*?**
		Tell me about more things you do at the weekend.	*I go shopping.* *I visit my grandparents.*	**Do you *go shopping*? Do you *visit your grandparents*?**
		OK, thank you, *. **Goodbye.**	**Goodbye.**	

* Remember to use the child's name throughout the test.

Test 2 Answers

Listening

Jane   Peter   Paul   Jim

Nick   Mary   Daisy

Part 1 (5 marks)

Lines should be drawn between:

1 Nick and the boy standing on the rock, fishing
2 Mary and the girl with fair hair, swimming
3 Peter and the boy trying to get the kite in the tree
4 Daisy and the girl by the door of the house, with the dog
5 Jane and the girl sitting in the boat, with a frog on her T-shirt

Part 2 (5 marks)

1 12/twelve   **2** carrots   **3** box
4 grey/gray (and) white / white (and) grey/gray
5 Hoppy (correct spelling)

Part 3 (5 marks)

1 Saturday – party, people dancing in the streets
2 Wednesday – zoo for sea animals, dolphins
3 Friday – film on television
4 Thursday – Grandma's garden, watermelons
5 Sunday – swam under water with Dad, fish

red
orange
blue
yellow

Part 4 (5 marks)

1 B   **2** A   **3** C   **4** B   **5** A

Part 5 (5 marks)

1 Colour the sandwich in the child's hand – blue
2 Colour the sweater on the bag – orange
3 Draw a ball in the sea
4 Colour the shell on the beach – yellow
5 Colour the father's face – red

TRANSCRIPT   *Hello. This is the Cambridge Movers Practice Listening Test, Test 2.*

Part 1   *Look at Part 1. Look at the picture. Listen and look. There is one example.*

[pause]

BOY: Look! This is a photo of my aunt's house. My eight cousins live there!
WOMAN: That's a lot of children!
BOY: Yes! There's Jim. He's the oldest. He's in the boat. He's wearing his football scarf.
WOMAN: In hot weather?
BOY: Yes!

[pause]

Can you see the line? This is an example. Now you listen and draw lines.

[pause]

1

WOMAN: What's the name of the boy who's standing on the rock?
BOY: Oh, that's Nick. He loves fishing.
WOMAN: Did he catch a fish that day?
BOY: No! He never catches any, but he likes trying.

[pause]

2

WOMAN: And who's the girl in the water?
BOY: Do you mean Mary? The girl who's got fair hair?
WOMAN: Yes. That's right.
BOY: She loves swimming.

[pause]

3

WOMAN: And there's someone in the tree. What's he doing?
BOY: Oh, that's Peter. He's trying to get his kite.
WOMAN: Was it a windy day, then?
BOY: Yes, it was.

[pause]

4

BOY: And can you see Daisy?
WOMAN: Which one is she?
BOY: She's by the door of the house with their dog. She's throwing something in the river for him.
WOMAN: Did the dog jump in?
BOY: Yes. He swims very well!

[pause]

5

BOY: And my youngest cousin is Jane.
WOMAN: And where's she?
BOY: She's sitting in the back of the boat.
WOMAN: She's got a frog on her T-shirt!
BOY: I know. I gave it to her.

[pause]

Now listen to Part 1 again.

[The recording is repeated.]

[pause]

That is the end of Part 1.

[pause]

Part 2 *Listen and look. There is one example.*

[pause]

GIRL: Excuse me, Mrs Wright.
WOMAN: Yes, Jill. What's the matter?
GIRL: Nothing, but can I ask you about your rabbit? I'd like to buy a pet but I can't choose. Where did you buy your rabbit?
WOMAN: At the pet shop.

[pause]

Can you see the answer? Now you listen and write.

[pause]

1

GIRL: How old is your rabbit now, Mrs Wright?
WOMAN: It's only twelve weeks old.
GIRL: Twelve weeks! It's very young!
WOMAN: Yes, but it eats a lot!

[pause]

2

GIRL: So, what's its favourite food? Does it like fruit?
WOMAN: Well, it does, but it likes carrots best.
GIRL: So do you buy carrots for it every day?
WOMAN: No. I buy a lot at the weekend.

[pause]

3

GIRL: And where does it sleep?
WOMAN: It sleeps in a box outside.
GIRL: Oh! Isn't it cold in the garden?
WOMAN: Yes, but it's OK inside the box.

[pause]

4

GIRL: And what colour is your rabbit?
WOMAN: Well, I wanted a brown one, but they only had grey and white ones.
GIRL: So what did you buy?
WOMAN: A grey and white one with very long ears.

[pause]

5

GIRL: And can you play with it?
WOMAN: Yes! It likes to jump and run in the garden.
GIRL: What's its name?
WOMAN: Hoppy.
GIRL: Is that H-O-P-P-Y?
WOMAN: Yes!

[pause]

Now listen to Part 2 again.

[The recording is repeated.]

[pause]

That is the end of Part 2.

[pause]

Part 3 *Look at the pictures. What did Vicky do last week?*
Listen and look. There is one example.

[pause]

MAN: OK, children. Last week, there was no school. What did you do, Vicky?
GIRL: I went to my grandma's house, Mr Banks. We went there on Monday.
MAN: Doesn't she live by the sea?
GIRL: Yes. We had to catch a train. I enjoyed that a lot!

[pause]

Can you see the line from the word Monday? On Monday, Vicky went on a train.
Now you listen and draw lines.

[pause]

1

GIRL:	On Saturday, there was a party in the village.
MAN:	Why?
GIRL:	I don't know. But there was music and all the people danced in the streets. There was a lot of food to eat on long tables too.
MAN:	Did you enjoy it?
GIRL:	Yes, I did.

[pause]

2

GIRL:	Wednesday was good ...
MAN:	Did you go swimming that day?
GIRL:	No. We went to a kind of zoo for sea animals and fish.
MAN:	What did you see there?
GIRL:	A lot of different things. I liked the dolphins best!

[pause]

3

GIRL:	But we didn't go out every day.
MAN:	Why not?
GIRL:	Well, on Friday it rained all day, and Mum didn't want to go outside.
MAN:	So what did you do?
GIRL:	There was a good film on television and we watched that.

[pause]

4

GIRL:	Another day, we worked in my grandma's garden.
MAN:	When was that?
GIRL:	On Thursday, I think. Yes, that's right. It was Thursday.
MAN:	And what's she got in her garden?
GIRL:	Oh ... a lot of flowers ... and potatoes, tomatoes and big green watermelons.

[pause]

5

MAN:	How about Sunday? Did you help your grandmother in her garden again that day?
GIRL:	No, I didn't. We went to the beach because it was so sunny.
MAN:	Did you go swimming that day then?
GIRL:	Yes. I swam under the water with my dad. We saw lots of different fish.
MAN:	Great!

[pause]

Now listen to Part 3 again.

[The recording is repeated.]

[pause]

That is the end of Part 3.

[pause]

Part 4 *Look at the pictures. Listen and look. There is one example.*

[pause]

Where's the new DVD?

[pause]

WOMAN:	Jane, go and find my new DVD, please. I'd like to watch it.
GIRL:	Where is it? Next to the television or in your bag?
WOMAN:	It's upstairs by the computer. I put it there this morning.
GIRL:	OK.

[pause]

Can you see the tick? Now you listen and tick the box.

[pause]

1 *Which book did John buy?*

BOY:	It was difficult to choose which book to buy.
WOMAN:	Yes. The one about the weather was good.
BOY:	And I liked the one about plants.
WOMAN:	But you chose the best one, I think. That book about music is very good.
BOY:	Yes, I could only buy one, and that one was best.

[pause]

2 *What does Sally want to do?*

MAN:	Sally, would you like to go sailing with me this afternoon?
GIRL:	Not today, Dad. Can we go shopping? I need a new dress.
MAN:	I don't want to go to town. How about skating?
GIRL:	No, I don't want to do that, Dad. Sorry!

[pause]

3 *What's in the playground?*

BOY:	What are you looking at, Miss?
WOMAN:	There's a coat on the ground outside, in the playground. Look.
BOY:	No, Miss, it's a blanket.
WOMAN:	Oh, yes. I need some new glasses! Go and pick it up please, Fred.

[pause]

4 *What's Ben drawing?*

MAN:	I like your drawing of a parrot, Ben! But its head is too small.
BOY:	It isn't a bird, Dad!
MAN:	What is it, then?
BOY:	It's a bat, Dad. Can't you see?
MAN:	Oh, yes!

[pause]

5 What's Mum doing?

GIRL:	Where's Mum? Is she cooking dinner?
MAN:	No. She's talking on the phone, I think.
GIRL:	Not now, she isn't.
MAN:	Oh, I know. She's having a shower.

[pause]

Now listen to Part 4 again.

[The recording is repeated.]

[pause]

That is the end of Part 4.

[pause]

Part 5 *Look at the picture. Listen and look. There is one example.*

[pause]

BOY:	Can I colour this picture of the beach now?
WOMAN:	Yes. It's very hot, I think! Can you see the book next to the man's feet?
BOY:	Yes. Shall I colour it?
WOMAN:	Yes, colour the book pink, please.
BOY:	All right.

[pause]

Can you see the pink book? This is an example.
Now you listen and colour and draw.

[pause]

1

WOMAN:	The child has a sandwich in his hand. Look!
BOY:	Oh, yes. Shall I colour it blue?
WOMAN:	A sandwich?
BOY:	Yes! Why not?
WOMAN:	OK.

[pause]

2

WOMAN:	Can you find the sweater which is on the bag? Colour that for me, please.
BOY:	OK. How about orange?
WOMAN:	Yes. That's a good sunny colour.
BOY:	Yes, it is. Right, I'm colouring that sweater now.
WOMAN:	Great!

[pause]

3

WOMAN:	Would you like to draw something?
BOY:	Yes. I'd like to draw something in the sea, please.
WOMAN:	All right. How about a ball in the sea?
BOY:	Yes, OK, a ball then.
WOMAN:	That's great!

[pause]

4

WOMAN:	Look at that shell! Can you see it?
BOY:	The one by the water on the beach? It's a kind of animal.
WOMAN:	Yes. Can you colour that shell yellow?
BOY:	Right. I'm doing that now.

[pause]

5

WOMAN:	And now, can you see the father's face?
BOY:	Yes. He's sleeping.
WOMAN:	You're right. Colour his face red.
BOY:	Because of the sun! All right. I love that colour!
WOMAN:	Good!

[pause]

Now listen to Part 5 again.

[The recording is repeated.]

[pause]

That is the end of the Movers Practice Listening Test 2.

Reading and Writing

Part 1 (6 marks)

1 a clown   2 a mountain   3 a farmer
4 a pirate   5 a jungle   6 a supermarket

Part 2 (6 marks)

1 yes   2 no   3 no   4 yes   5 yes   6 yes

Part 3 (6 marks)

1 C   2 C   3 A   4 B   5 A   6 B

Part 4 (7 marks)

1 shouts   2 bedroom   3 computers   4 stars
5 swims   6 dancing   7 My family

Part 5 (10 marks)

1 flat/home/apartment   2 video   3 go to town
4 map   5 (pictures of) whales   6 long (and
white)/white (and long)   7 Peter   8 (Aunt) Sue
9 (blue) bag   10 the island/Whale Island

Part 6 (5 marks)

1 out   2 but   3 Its   4 than   5 sit

Speaking

Part	Examiner does this:	Examiner says this:	Minimum response expected from child:	Back-up questions:
	Usher brings candidate in.	Usher to examiner: **Hello. This is (child's name*).** Examiner: **Hello, *. My name's Jane/Ms Smith.** **How old are you, *?**	Hello. *nine*	 **Are you nine/ten?**
1	Points to **Find the differences** pictures.	**Look at these pictures. They look the same, but some things are different. Here there are three people, but here there are four.** **What other different things can you see?**	Describes four other differences: • purple/yellow scarf • leaves/no leaves • number 46/73 • rabbit/frog	Point to other differences the candidate does not mention. Give first half of response: **Here the boy's scarf is purple, but here ...**
2	Points to **Picture Story**. Allows time to look at the pictures.	**Now look at these pictures. They show a story. It's called 'A windy day'. Just look at the pictures first. (Pause.) Look at the first one.** **Peter and his mother are walking in the street. It's very windy.** **Now you tell the story.** (pointing at the other pictures)	(Many variations possible) **Peter's hat's going into the tree.** **Peter's climbing the tree.** **He can see his hat now. A bird's wearing it.**	 Questions to prompt other parts of the story: **Where's Peter's hat going?** **What's Peter doing?** **Can Peter see his hat now?**

* Remember to use the child's name throughout the test.

Part	Examiner does this:	Examiner says this:	Minimum response expected from child:	Back-up questions:
3	Points to the **Odd-one-out** pictures.	**Now look at these four pictures. One is different. The book is different. A lemon, a pineapple and an orange are fruit. You eat them. You don't eat a book. You read it.**		
	Points to the second, third and fourth sets of pictures in turn.	**Now you tell me about these pictures. Which one is different? (Why?)**	Candidate suggests a difference (any plausible difference is acceptable).	**What are these people doing?** (dancing) **And these people?** (swimming)
				These men all have a … ? (moustache) **And this man?** (no moustache)
				What do you have in these? (drinks) **And in this?** (pencils)
4	Puts away all pictures.	**Now let's talk about your English classes.**		
		What day do you have your English class?	*Monday*	**Do you have your English class on *Monday*?**
		Who do you sit next to?	*(my) friend*	**Do you sit next to *your friend*?**
		Is English difficult or easy?	*easy*	**Is English *easy*?**
		Tell me about your English teacher.	*Her/His name's …*	**What's your English teacher's name?**
			He/She gives us lots of homework.	**Does he/she give you lots of homework?**
		OK, thank you, *. Goodbye.	*Goodbye.*	

* Remember to use the child's name throughout the test.

Test 3 Answers

Listening

Part 1 (5 marks)

Lines should be drawn between:

1 Vicky and the woman playing the piano
2 Jack and the boy in a tree, with a dolphin on his T-shirt
3 Jane and the girl dancing, with long hair
4 Fred and the boy under the table, playing with the kitten
5 Paul and the boy in the lion's costume, with a tail

Part 2 (5 marks)

1 pirates   2 Pound (correct spelling)   3 bus
4 home (on the computer)   5 Pat

Part 3 (5 marks)

1 Tuesday – house for baby sheep
2 Monday – sailing
3 Friday – baby sheep in field
4 Thursday – walk by lake
5 Wednesday – read books inside

Part 4 (5 marks)

1 C   2 B   3 A   4 B   5 A

Part 5 (5 marks)

1 Colour the star outside the window – yellow
2 Colour the sweater on the floor – orange
3 Write 'ALEX' on the end of the bed by the boy's feet
4 Colour the lamp above the boy's head – purple
5 Colour the shell in the fish bowl – blue

TRANSCRIPT   *Hello. This is the Cambridge Movers Practice Listening Test, Test 3.*

Part 1   *Look at Part 1. Look at the picture. Listen and look. There is one example.*

[pause]

BOY: We had a great party last weekend in our garden, Miss Page.
WOMAN: Did you? In the afternoon?
BOY: No, in the evening. Some of the people wore funny clothes. But my brother Peter didn't. Look, he's there with a guitar.
WOMAN: Oh, yes! He's got red hair like you!

[pause]

Can you see the line? This is an example.
Now you listen and draw lines.

[pause]

1

WOMAN: Who's playing the piano? Is that your mother?
BOY: No. It's a friend of ours. Her name's Vicky.
WOMAN: I see. Is she good at playing the piano?
BOY: Yes, she's great!

[pause]

2

WOMAN: Who's that in the tree?
BOY: That's my brother's friend, Jack.
WOMAN: Oh … and what's that on his T-shirt?
BOY: It's a dolphin, I think.

[pause]

3

BOY: And there's Jane … she danced like that all night!
WOMAN: Do you mean the girl with the long hair?
BOY: Yes. She's one of our cousins.
WOMAN: How many cousins have you got?
BOY: Only two.

[pause]

4

BOY: My other cousin's under the table. His name's Fred. Look!
WOMAN: Oh, yes! But why is he there?
BOY: He loves playing with our black kitten.
WOMAN: I can see that!

[pause]

5

WOMAN: And what about the person with the lion's face? Who's that?
BOY: Oh, that's Paul. He lives in the house next to ours.
WOMAN: Did he paint his face like that?
BOY: No. My sister did it for him.
WOMAN: And he's got a tail too!
BOY: Yes. He looked very funny.

[pause]

Now listen to Part 1 again.

[The recording is repeated.]

[pause]

That is the end of Part 1.

[pause]

Part 2   *Listen and look. There is one example.*

[pause]

GIRL: Can we go to the cinema today, Dad?
MAN: Ermm … yes. I think that's OK. Which film do you want to see?
GIRL: It's called 'Treasure'. It's great! Lucy told me.
MAN: 'Treasure'? OK, we can go this afternoon.
GIRL: Thanks!

[pause]

Can you see the answer? Now you listen and write.

[pause]

1

MAN: What's the film about?
GIRL: It's about pirates. It's very exciting.
MAN: Pirates?
GIRL: Yes. I love that kind of story.

[pause]

2

MAN: Which cinema is it at?
GIRL: The one in Pound Street. I can spell that word. I learnt it at school.
MAN: Is it P-O-U-N-D?
GIRL: Yes, that's right, Dad. Well done!

[pause]

3

GIRL: How can we go there? Can you drive us there in the car?
MAN: The bus is quicker, I think.
GIRL: Mmm.
MAN: Yes, let's take the bus. It's easier, too.

[pause]

4

GIRL: What about the tickets? We can buy them at the cinema.
MAN: No. Let's buy them at home. We can do that on the new computer.
GIRL: At home? Good idea. Let's do that now.
MAN: OK.

[pause]

5

MAN: And would you like to take a friend with you?
GIRL: Oh, yes. Can I invite Pat to come with us?
MAN: Yes! Go and ask her now.
GIRL: Great. Thanks, Dad. Pat loves going to the cinema.

[pause]

Now listen to Part 2 again.

[The recording is repeated.]

[pause]

That is the end of Part 2.

[pause]

Part 3   *Look at the pictures. What did John do last week? Listen and look. There is one example.*

[pause]

WOMAN: Did you go and see your friend on the farm last week, John?
BOY: Yes, Miss Best. I went on the train. It was exciting.

WOMAN: Good. What day was that?
BOY: I went on Sunday. Jim, that's my friend, and his parents came to the station to get me.

[pause]

Can you see the line from the word Sunday? On Sunday, John went by train to see his friend, Jim. Now you listen and draw lines.

[pause]

1

BOY: There's lots of work to do on the farm.
WOMAN: What did you do there?
BOY: Well, on Tuesday, Jim and I made a kind of house for the baby sheep.
WOMAN: Was that difficult?
BOY: Yes! I was tired on Tuesday evening, but it was a lot of fun.

[pause]

2

WOMAN: But what did you do on Monday? More work?
BOY: No, we went sailing at Jim's school.
WOMAN: But it's the school holidays.
BOY: I know. We went because Jim's learning to sail and there's a lake there.

[pause]

3

BOY: Friday was a good day too.
WOMAN: What did you do that day?
BOY: We went to the fields with Jim's dad to see the baby sheep again. I gave one some milk.
WOMAN: What did you do then?
BOY: We chose names for them all.

[pause]

4

WOMAN: And what did you do on Thursday?
BOY: Thursday? We took the cows to a new field. Then we went for a walk by the lake.
WOMAN: Did you go sailing that day too?
BOY: No. It was too windy.

[pause]

5

BOY: It rained and rained one day.
WOMAN: Was that Saturday? It was very wet here that day.
BOY: No, it was Wednesday. But they've got lots of books there. We read and played games inside.

WOMAN: What did you read about?
BOY: Three children and their father who drives a train. The person who wrote it lives in Jim's village.
WOMAN: Wow!

[pause]

Now listen to Part 3 again.

[The recording is repeated.]

[pause]

That is the end of Part 3.

[pause]

Part 4 *Look at the pictures. Listen and look. There is one example.*

[pause]

What's Mary making?

[pause]

MAN: Mary! Are you in the kitchen?
GIRL: Yes, Dad.
MAN: Are you making some sandwiches?
GIRL: No … a cup of tea for Mum.
MAN: Oh, good. And can you get me an ice cream, please?
GIRL: OK.

[pause]

Can you see the tick? Now you listen and tick the box.

[pause]

1 What's the weather like this morning?

MAN: Hmmm. I'd like to go for a long walk this morning.
WOMAN: But it's raining!
MAN: I know. Yesterday was sunny, but I wanted to watch the football on the television …
WOMAN: Well, I don't want to come with you. It's not windy, but it's too cold for me.

[pause]

2 Where are Nick's shoes now?

BOY: Mum, I can't find my shoes. They were in my bedroom. Where are they now? Do you know?
WOMAN: Yes. I put them in the garden, Nick. You need to clean them. They're very dirty.
BOY: OK. Where can I do it?
WOMAN: In the hall.

[pause]

3 Who's going to the shops with Daisy?

MAN: Hello, Daisy. Where are you now?
GIRL: Hello, Dad. I'm going to the shops.
MAN: Are you? With Mum?
GIRL: No. With Grandpa. We have to get a present for my friend in my class at school.
MAN: Which friend?
GIRL: Tom.

[pause]

4 What's inside the cage?

BOY: Oh, look! What's that inside this cage? Is it a lizard?
GIRL: No, they don't look like that. Is it a kind of snake?
BOY: No, it's not. Oh, look! It's a bat!
GIRL: Wow! I never saw one of those before.

[pause]

5 How old is Sally's grandmother?

GIRL: It was my grandmother's birthday last Monday.
BOY: Was it, Sally? My grandfather's birthday was last week too. He was sixty-four – sorry, I mean sixty-five.
GIRL: Well, my grandmother's younger than that. She's only fifty-seven.
BOY: Does she live near you, Sally?
GIRL: Yes, she does.

[pause]

Now listen to Part 4 again.

[The recording is repeated.]

[pause]

That is the end of Part 4.

[pause]

Part 5 *Look at the picture. Listen and look. There is one example.*

[pause]

MAN: Can you colour some of this picture now, please?
GIRL: Yes! Is the boy having a dream in this picture?
MAN: Yes, he is. He's flying, look! Like the birds in his book.
GIRL: Wow! Can I colour the river in his dream?
MAN: Yes, colour the river green.
GIRL: OK.

[pause]

Can you see the green river? This is an example.

Now you listen and colour and write.

[pause]

1

GIRL: I can see a star outside. Can I colour that star now?
MAN: Yes. Good idea! What colour do you want?
GIRL: I've got a yellow pencil here. Is that colour OK?
MAN: Yes. That's fine.

[pause]

2

GIRL: And can I colour the boy's sweater?
MAN: OK. Colour the sweater that's on the floor. Make it orange.
GIRL: All right. I can do that now.
MAN: Good.

[pause]

3

MAN: Now, would you like to write something in this picture?
GIRL: Yes! What must I write?
MAN: Write 'Alex' on the end of the bed by the boy's feet.
GIRL: Why must I write 'Alex'?
MAN: Because that's the boy's name.

[pause]

4

GIRL: Can I colour the lamp now?
MAN: Yes. Colour the one that's above the boy's head. Colour it purple.
GIRL: OK. I like that lamp. I've got one like that.
MAN: Have you?
GIRL: Yes.

[pause]

5

MAN: Now, find the shell.
GIRL: Which one? There are two in this picture.
MAN: Colour the shell that's in the bowl. Make it blue.
GIRL: All right! Mmmm. I'm tired now too!
MAN: Well, that's the end!

[pause]

Now listen to Part 5 again.

[The recording is repeated.]

[pause]

That is the end of the Movers Practice Listening Test 3.

Reading and Writing

Part 1 (6 marks)

1 a shower   **2** feet   **3** a beard   **4** a balcony
5 a shoulder   **6** mountains

Part 2 (6 marks)

1 no   **2** no   **3** no   **4** no   **5** yes   **6** yes

Part 3 (6 marks)

1 C   **2** B   **3** C   **4** B   **5** C   **6** A

Part 4 (7 marks)

1 cooked   **2** basement   **3** laugh   **4** presents
5 camera   **6** watched   **7** Grandma's exciting day

Part 5 (10 marks)

1 (very) naughty   **2** kitchen   **3** bowl (of water)
4 (very) hungry   **5** cat's   **6** lemon   **7** ball
8 (very) boring   **9** sleep   **10** food (and praise)

Part 6 (5 marks)

1 or   **2** There   **3** after   **4** their   **5** is

Speaking

Part	Examiner does this:	Examiner says this:	Minimum response expected from child:	Back-up questions:
	Usher brings candidate in.	Usher to examiner: **Hello. This is (child's name*).** Examiner: **Hello, *. My name's** *Jane/Ms Smith.* **How old are you, *?**	Hello. *nine*	**Are you** *nine/ten***?**
1	Points to **Find the differences** pictures.	**Look at these pictures. They look the same, but some things are different. This farmer has a moustache, but this farmer doesn't.** **What other different things can you see?**	Describes four other differences: • 5/4 cows • rabbit/cat • green/yellow plants • cloudy/sunny	Point to other differences the candidate does not mention. Give first half of response: **Here there are five cows, but here ...**
2	Points to **Picture Story**. Allows time to look at the pictures.	**Now look at these pictures. They show a story. It's called 'Vicky, Jack and the baby'. Just look at the pictures first. (Pause.) Look at the first one.** **Vicky and Jack are at home. They're singing and playing the guitar. Their mum's saying, 'Please be quiet. The baby must go to sleep now.'** **Now you tell the story.** (pointing at the other pictures)	(Many variations possible) *Vicky and Jack are reading.* *The baby's crying.* *Vicky and Jack aren't happy.* *Now the children are singing a song for the baby.* *The baby's sleeping. Mum is surprised and happy.*	Questions to prompt other parts of the story: **What are Vicky and Jack doing?** **What's the baby doing?** **What are the children doing now?** **What's the baby doing now?**

* Remember to use the child's name throughout the test.

Part	Examiner does this:	Examiner says this:	Minimum response expected from child:	Back-up questions:
3	Points to **Odd-one-out** pictures.	**Now look at these four pictures. One is different. The book is different. A lemon, a pineapple and an orange are fruit. You eat them. You don't eat a book. You read it.**		
	Points to the second, third and fourth sets of pictures in turn.	**Now you tell me about these pictures. Which one is different? (Why?)**	Candidate suggests a difference (any plausible difference is acceptable).	**These are all ... ?** (square) **And this is ... ?** (round) **What can these do?** (fly) **And this?** (jump) **These are all ... ?** (clothes) **And this is a ... ?** (ruler)
4	Puts away all pictures.	**Now let's talk about food.**		
		What is your favourite fruit?	*apple(s)*	**Do you like *apples*?**
		Who cooks in your house?	*my mum*	**Does your *mum* cook?**
		Where do you eat lunch?	*(at) school*	**Do you eat lunch *at school*?**
		Tell me about the things you eat at weekends.	*We eat burgers and chips/fries.* *We eat cakes.*	**Do you eat *burgers and chips/fries*? Do you eat *cakes*?**
		OK, thank you, *. **Goodbye.**	**Goodbye.**	

* Remember to use the child's name throughout the test.

COMBINED STARTERS AND MOVERS THEMATIC VOCABULARY LIST

For ease of reference, vocabulary is arranged in semantic groups or themes. Some words appear under more than one heading.

In addition to the topics, notions and concepts listed for the syllabus, the following categories appear:

- useful words and expressions
- adjectives
- pronouns
- determiners
- verbs
- adverbs
- modals
- prepositions
- question words
- conjunctions
- names

s – first appears at *Starters*
m – first appears at *Movers*

ANIMALS

s animal
m bat
m bear
s bird
m cage
s cat
s chicken
s cow
s crocodile
s dog
m dolphin
s duck
s elephant
s fish (s & pl)
m fly
s frog
s giraffe
s goat
s hippo
s horse
m kangaroo
m kitten
m lion
s lizard
s monkey
s mouse/mice
m panda
m parrot
m pet
m puppy
m rabbit
m shark
s sheep (s & pl)
s snake
s spider
s tail
s tiger
m whale
s zoo

THE BODY & FACE

s arm
m back
m beard
m blond(e)
s body
m curly
s ear
s eye
s face
m fair
s foot/feet
s hair
s hand
s head
s leg
m moustache
s mouth
m neck
s nose
m shoulder
s smile
m stomach
m straight
m tooth/teeth

CLOTHES

s bag
s clothes
m coat
s dress

s glasses
s handbag
s hat
s jacket
s jeans
m scarf
s shirt
s shoe
s skirt
s sock
m sweater
s trousers
s T-shirt
s watch
s wear

COLOURS

s black
s blue
s brown
s green
s grey (or gray)
s orange
s pink
s purple
s red
s white
s yellow

FAMILY & FRIENDS

m aunt
s baby
s boy
s brother
s child/children
s cousin

s dad(dy)
m daughter
s family
s father
s friend
s girl
m granddaughter
s grandfather
s grandma
s grandmother
s grandpa
m grandparent
m grandson
m grown up
s live
s man/men
s Miss
s mother
s Mr
s Mrs
s mum(my)
s old
m parent
s person/people
s sister
m son
s their
s them
s they
m uncle
s us
s we
s woman/women
s you
s young
s your

FOOD & DRINK

s apple
s banana
s bean
m bottle
m bowl
s bread
s breakfast
s burger
s cake
s carrot
m cheese
s chicken
s chips (US fries)
s coconut
m coffee
m cup
s dinner
s drink (n & v)
s eat

s egg
s fish
s food
s fries (UK chips)
s fruit
m glass of
s grape
m hungry
s ice cream
s juice
s lemon
s lemonade
s lime
s lunch
s mango
s meat
s milk
s onion
s orange
m pasta
s pea
s pear
m picnic
s pineapple
s potato
s rice
m salad
m sandwich
s sausage
m soup
s supper
m tea
m thirsty
s tomato
m vegetable
s water
s watermelon

HEALTH

m cold
m cough
m doctor
m earache
m fine
m headache
m hospital
m hurt
m matter (What's the matter?)
m nurse
m stomach-ache
m temperature
m toothache

THE HOME

m address
s apartment

s armchair
m balcony
m basement
s bath
s bathroom
s bed
s bedroom
m blanket
s bookcase
s box
s camera
s chair
s clock
s computer
s cupboard
s desk
s dining room
s doll
s door
m downstairs
m dream
m elevator
m fan
s flat
s floor
s flower
s garden
s hall
m home
s house
s kitchen
s lamp
m lift
s living room
s mat
s mirror
s painting
s phone
s picture
s radio
s room
m shopping
m shower
s sleep
s sofa
m stair(s)
s table
s television/TV
m toothbrush
m towel
s toy
s tree
m upstairs
s wall
m wash (n & v)
s watch
s window

NUMBERS

s Cardinals: 1–20
m Cardinals: 21–100
m Ordinals: 1st–20th

PLACES & DIRECTIONS

m above
m bank
s behind
s between
m bus station
m café
m cinema
m farm
s here
m hospital
s in
s in front of
m library
m map
m market
s next to
s on
s park
m place
m playground
m road
s shop (US store)
m square
s store (UK shop)
m straight
s street
m supermarket
m swimming pool
s there
s under
s zoo

SCHOOL

s alphabet
s answer
s ask
s board
s book
s bookcase
s class
s classroom
s close
s colour
s computer
s correct
s cross
s cupboard
s desk
s door
s draw(ing)

s English
s eraser
s example
s find
s floor
m homework
s know
s learn
s lesson
s letter (as in alphabet)
s line
s listen (to)
s look
m mistake
s name
s number
s open
s page
s part
s pen
s pencil
s picture
s playground
s question
s read
s right (as in correct)
s rubber
s ruler
s school
s sentence
s spell
s stand (up)
s story
s teacher
s tell
s test (n & v)
m text
s tick (n & v)
s understand
s wall
s window
s word
s write

SPORTS & LEISURE

s badminton
s ball
s baseball
s basketball
m bat
s beach
s bike
s boat
s book
s bounce
s camera
s catch

m CD
m comic/comic book
s doll
s draw(ing)
s drive (v)
m DVD
s enjoy
s favourite
m film
s fish(ing)
s fly
s football (US soccer)
s game
s guitar
s hit
s hobby
s hockey
m holiday
s jump
s kick (v)
m kick (n)
s kite
s listen (to)
m movie
m music
s paint(ing)
m party
s photo
s piano
s picture
s play (with)
m present
s radio
s read
s ride (n & v)
s run
m sail
s sing
m skate
s soccer (UK football)
s song
s sport
m sports centre
s story
m swim (n)
m swimming pool
s table tennis
s television/TV
s tennis
s throw
m towel
s toy
s TV/television
m video
m walk (n)
s watch

TIME

m after
s afternoon
m age
m always
m before
s birthday
s clock
s day
s end
s evening
m every
s morning
m never
s night
m sometimes
s today
s watch
m week
m weekend
m yesterday
   The days of the week:
m Sunday
m Monday
m Tuesday
m Wednesday
m Thursday
m Friday
m Saturday

TOYS

s ball
s baseball
s basketball
s bike
s car
s doll
s football
s game
s helicopter
s kite
s lorry (US truck)
s monster
s plane
s robot
s toy
s train
m treasure
s truck (UK lorry)

TRANSPORT

s bike
s boat
s bus
m bus station
s car
m drive
m driver
s fly
s go
s helicopter
s lorry (US truck)
s motorbike
s plane
s ride
s run
s swim
m ticket
s train
s truck (UK lorry)
s walk

WEATHER

m cloud
m cloudy
m rain
m rainbow
m snow
s sun
m sunny
m weather
m wind
m windy

WORK

m clown
m doctor
m farmer
m hospital
m nurse
m pirate
s teacher
m work

THE WORLD AROUND US

s beach
m city
m country(side)
m field
m forest
m grass
m ground
m island
m jungle
m lake
m leaf/leaves
m moon
m mountain
m plant
m river
m road
m rock
s sand
s sea
s shell
m star
s street
s sun
m town
s tree
m village
s water
m waterfall
m world

USEFUL WORDS & EXPRESSIONS

s bye (-bye)
m come on!
m excuse me
s goodbye
s hello
s I don't know
s no
s oh
s oh dear
s OK
s pardon
s please
s right
m see you!
s so
s sorry
s thank you
s thanks
s then
s well
s well done
s wow
s yes

ADJECTIVES

m afraid
m all
m all right
s angry
m awake
m back
m bad
s beautiful
m best
m better
s big
m boring
m bottom
m busy
m careful
s clean
m clever

s closed
m cloudy
m cold
s correct
m different
m difficult
s dirty
s double
m easy
s English
m every
m exciting
m famous
m fat
s favourite
m fine
m first
s funny
s good
s great
s happy
s her
s his
m hot
m hungry
s its
m last
s long
m loud
m more
m most
s my
m naughty
s new
s nice
s old
s our
m quick
m quiet
s right (correct)
m round
s sad
m second
s short
m slow
s small
s sorry
m square
m straight
m strong
m surprised
m tall
m terrible
s their
m thin
m third
m thirsty
m tired

m top
s ugly
m weak
m well
m wet
m windy
m worse
m worst
m wrong
s young
s your

DETERMINERS

s a/an
m all
s a lot of
m another
m any
m both
m every
s lots of
s many
m more
m most
s my
s no
s one
s some
s that
s the
s these
s this
s those

ADVERBS

s a lot
s again
m all right
m always
m back
m badly
m best
m better
m carefully
m down
m downstairs
m first
s here
m how
m how much
m how often
m inside
m last
s lots
m loudly
m more
m most

m near
m never
s not
s now
m off
m often
m on
m only
m out
m outside
m quickly
m quietly
m round
m slowly
m sometimes
s then
s there
s today
s too
m up
m upstairs
s very
m well
m when
m worse
m worst
m yesterday

PREPOSITIONS

s about
m above
m after
s at
m before
s behind
m below
s between
m by
m down
s for
s from
s in (prep of place)
m in (prep of time)
s in front of
m inside
s like
m near
s next to
s of
m off
s on (prep of place)
m on (prep of time)
m opposite
m out of
m outside
m round
m than
s to

s under
m up
s with

CONJUNCTIONS

s and
m because
s but
s or
m than
m when

PRONOUNS

m all
m another
m both
s he
s her
s hers
s him
s his
s I
s it
s its
s me
s mine
m more
m most
m nothing
s one
s ours
s she
m something
s that
s theirs
s them
s these
s they
s this
s those
s us
s we
m which
m who
s you
s yours

VERBS

Irregular:

s be
m bring
m buy
s catch (a ball)
m catch (a bus)
s choose
s come
s do
s draw

s drink
s drive
s eat
s find
s fly
s get
m get (un)dressed
m get up
s give
s go
m go shopping
s have
s have (got)
m have (got) to
m hide
s hit
s hold
m hurt
s know
s learn
m lose
s make
m mean
m must
s put
m put on
s read
s ride
s run
s say
s see
s sing
s sit (down)
s sleep
s spell
s stand (up)
s swim
m take
m take (a bus)
s take (a photo)
m take off
s tell
m think
s throw
s understand
m wake up
s wear
s write

Regular:

s add
s answer
s ask
s bounce
m call
m carry
s clean
m climb
s close

s colour
s complete
m cook
s cross
m cry
m dance
m dream
m drop
m email
s enjoy
m film
m fish
m help
m hop
m invite
s jump
s kick
m laugh
s learn
s like
s listen (to)
s live
s look
s look at
m look for
s love
m move
m need
s open
s paint
s phone
s pick up
m plant
s play (with)
s point
m rain
m sail
m shop
m shout
s show
m skate
m skip
s smile
m snow
s start
s stop
s talk
s test
m text
s tick
s try
m video
m wait
s walk
s want
m wash
s watch
s wave
m work

MODALS

s　can/cannot/can't
m　could
m　must
m　shall
m　would

QUESTION WORDS

s　how
s　how many
m　how much
m　how often
s　how old
s　what
m　when
s　where
s　which
s　who
s　whose
m　why

NAMES

s　Alex
s　Ann
s　Anna
s　Ben
s　Bill
m　Daisy
m　Fred
m　Jack
m　Jane
s　Jill
m　Jim
m　John
s　Kim
s　Lucy
m　Mary
s　May
s　Nick
s　Pat
m　Paul
m　Peter
m　Sally
s　Sam
s　Sue
s　Tom
s　Tony
m　Vicky